Jen Currin
The Inquisition Yours

Coach House Books, Toronto

first edition

  Canada

Published with the generous assistance of the Canada Council for the Arts and the Ontario Arts Council. Coach House Books also acknowledges the support of the Government of Canada through the Book Publishing Industry Development Program and the Government of Ontario through the Ontario Book Publishing Tax Credit.

LIBRARY AND ARCHIVES CANADA CATALOGUING IN PUBLICATION

Currin, Jen
    The inquisition yours / Jen Currin.

Poems.
ISBN 978-1-55245-230-1

    I. Title.

PS8605.U77I67 2010   C811'.6   C2010-900030-7

for the teachers

'Magicians were and will always be my companions.'
– Giannina Braschi

Papers

SOCK MARTYRS

Black dress – I've already donated
my own death.

All the monkeys hide
inside the closet shrine.

No longer attached to our bodies
we glide over the fields.

How many times can we say *mountain*?
How many numb brides? Idols? Idle minds?

Used to be there was – god
with a big *g*.
Now countless songbirds
whenever the mirror is mentioned.

*

These changes are autobiographical –
at least, that's what I'm told.

Maimed in the way of fiction,
incalculable as the hot and cold hells,

but still – intimate.
We're glad to wake from it.

*

I hear the healer eating crackers
on the other side of her curtain.

Monks leave their tents
and stop to listen.

Her song has the flavour of tea
steeped too long.

One monk, myself,
broke his leg while motorcycling

and now leans against a fence,
flinching in the steep light.

*

It was thought that young children
should not be exposed to pregnancy.

I took my baby's dream
to the country of the assassin
and spoke with her assistant.

All vowels are owls and bread, wine.

In constant battle with my written self,
I had to agree.

*

Bottles smashed on heads,
men sawn in half.

Mother said we must quit this magic show.

Turn it into a vigilant knowledge –
A maimed army of lyricists

mimes the black and white laughter
of the fat man on television.

Buddha winks, tending his broken thumb.

'The Americans' wake from their trance,
suddenly melancholic –

it hurts
to jump from the steeple.

THE INQUISITION YOURS

My parents chose my name from a list.
They closed their eyes and pointed.

I rang my sister. We went running in the fields.

Entranced by lightning.
Starting each sentence with *So*.

I was a camera read to in the womb.

We were having ground flax seeds for breakfast.

Because my mother promised Buddha
not to kill.

Choose one adjective, my sister said.
As if I really could stand out

in the *savage* rain.

I was born four months later
in my uncle's apartment

overlooking the sea.

My sister's self-portrait perfected by rain.

It was a clear morning.
I had nothing planned for my body/the day.

Tomorrow night I will heal you with mint —

My sister's promise
to make up what she can't remember.

A hair's length, arm's width.
Resident. Resonant. Foolish.

I was read to in a red room.

Out of curiosity (not mine)

we got down on the floor and became cats together.

AMAZE

A childhood torn from clouds. I knew tigers. Grimace of thieves, appreciation of apprentices. Encyclopedias slept on, wept on. Significant non-others seized me from the dust and told me I was their city. Wide sleeves of a death unmade. Stealing orange juice, listening to my father's puns — to split the world in two. I learned metaphor before speech.

A chemical you told the time to.
Pour your coffee
in a jar, put it in your bag, pedal away.
In good January, I seek Wednesday's
bells. Greet a group of genetic experts.
I'll meet my maker anywhere:
in a foil wrapper, a toxic thyroid.
No, honey, I'm not.
I've never even been.
So take a good twist.
Whatever I write in this little book
will have the taste of you.
Tomorrow is an uncle or a magic beach.
We must face language, fancy it.
Seek a kind of alchemy –
Of public.
Of *take care of it.*
The goings are coming closer –
two years in a nocturnal
children's book. The crows
have stepped all over my face.

A NARRATIVE IN NEW BLUE JEANS

Then look to these quotes for questions.
The self-made scholar's philosophy exam.
I'm spiritual on Fridays,
keys all over the floor.

Keeping it concrete and hidden.
Someone gets a letter or a telephone call.
I'll say this now,
then go home and think differently.

Instant. Constant. Commodify.

Just to read them
making us small.

I'll be your friend
'by donation.'

Fanzine from an alien culture:
your wristwatch's picture.

The first ingredient is always sugar –
to prance around in, practically nude.

More and more bored with 'I' –
but what else?

The carriage came; we climbed on.

DRAGON

It was a holy stroll
through your old neighbourhood,
teens smoking in the trees.
A stoical man in a lab coat –
I think I hate your father.
It's a humble hatred that keeps me
in this second-hand red gown.

Eastern earrings, my daughter's terrifying
cellphone ring.
The underforest of any story
is me bittering my body with yours.
Some severe source of light, cliff
to climb in your eyes.
I was worried I'd forget things.
The old salmon woman's holy vulnerability –
Once I kissed a dragon where mist was ordinary.

BEFORE THE SHINE DULLS

I distrust narrative. The body's promise —
I'll be on top. Interiorly. The reason I believe —

There are acres, a fish I spent
my life waiting for.

Cold boys gamble in the morning.
I have a head that aches.

Verbs are something to hold on to.
I stroll, rumble, grip, wrench —

I won't be who you remember.
We'll masquerade as acquaintances
for a few blank moments.

                    *

My friend the painter in a dream
recommends a sexual position I've never tried.
I don't know what to tell him —
maybe that I was a woman yesterday
but parked that overnight.

Now I see through the bedroom window
my capacity for holding anger.

It is still dark out, and morning.

HALF-NAKED OR PARTIALLY CLOTHED

it's just chemistry – people
in a room

identical boxes

shoes that don't squeak

'friendship = sharing accomplishments'

I didn't find my accomplice that interesting

waiting for wine in a leatherette booth

the dictionary's crime

'my bicycle is in need of a good oiling'

sacrificing another story to sarcasm

I really did make myself dizzy
at the grief teleconference

my watch flashed in the sun

I combed a new grave,
restrung my bass –

all intimacies were dead

the sun had gone dark and gruesome

and it wasn't for laughter,
the only victim
of my enormous pity –

EVERYONE'S SILENCE

more sugar   I intend to feel

two stars compete for my attention

the whole photo

specifically a sister
putting sugar in her coffee

I was on wheels   redundant

gave you a fork   you needed a spoon

your eye on something   the death of our friendship

sent me a map of celestial schools
I was my own suitor

hotter, hungover

an orange you bit into

there are some good-looking women in this city

the way your teeth held my upper lip

our arms crossed
our words of broken clay

APRIL IMPERFECT, I COUGH ON MY MIRROR

I want to work for you, vampire.
Monday through Friday through fields —
warm water.

And it's sick what you talk about —
the ideal world.

To some degree, I disagree.

You can't do much in two days high-heeled.
I thrust myself upon them,
unsatisfied. You're still talking
Monday, Friday.

Some places are unconvincing.
Your smile. You have
the girl, I won't
begrudge you.

*

We fell here. We didn't do anything wrong.
We wanted capacity — a wing, a wing.
Paper clipped to my birth certificate —

We wanted an ideal world
(to some degree).

People I knew from childhood
change before death – a place so quiet
you can hear the cat cleaning herself.

HEARD

Genius is the word for *I've lost the job
and my heart is breakfast.*

Cat over moon and step where you please.
Please – I've applied myself

teaching horse-see-monkey-do.
It's ordinary to work at what we hate.

Dust by dust you accumulate a life.
The proof is running to market

with a pig under its arm
balled up like underwear.

I'm not so gaudy and can't love any better.
Who will I save next oh let me take a shower.

No gentler than my father.
I'm sorry he beat you and I'm sorry I didn't wake.

But of all the places my brother can be found
singing in his shrunken coat, I choose

your temple. Kiss your third eye.
For hardly ever is it granted so easily.

With effort, the word is *vulnerable*.
If the field must be divided, keep your shoes

and I'll take the motorcycle.
We're already more people than we were

this morning. By that I mean I'm frightened
of your inner children. Keep calling them puppies

and you'll starve.
I'm sorry about your grandmother.

When we're alone – that's it.
They kept calling us puppets

and it only matters now.

THE SHIVERS

Sea salt is whitest.
My name means *flower* and *air*.

I happened to meet this man
back from the holy city.

Our bodies broke the tension.

Two o'clock and it was coffee
ordered. My home
of flour and water.

When I was tired of him
I set his things outside the door.

This was called *divorce*.

He made a hundred clay boats
for his murdered father.

Borrowed a book from god's shelf.

Mischief of the holy city, whitest pig.
Only half my persona.

Cold mouse, non-luck,
quiescent sister.

We talked sailor,
one sweater in this world,

one foot in the next.

| A goodly weep as we unfastened our bells.

| Salt makers like ceramicists –

| I am familiar with the fear you describe.

CHAMPAGNE IN LOVE WITH THE NUMBER SEVEN

Dark inquiry – I've married
the jury.

Sister reads to children,
I light candles.

One shoe scratched by cousins,
one marble telling the floor.

She lowers the hours like a chandelier,

her heaven frequented by hysterics.
Innocent, experienced.

From the arch of her eyebrow/foot
I can guess it will be over in a topless second:

road, dolphins, meditation.

I linger with insects in the very depths of a bargain,

some small great garden.

STAINED PAPER, THE CURSE OF

coast barrelling into coast.

I've been there and back, never cured.

The festival's vagina always open.

Doubtless college would have done me good
but the night before admissions it rained

so I wrote my first list in the failing reason.
I could barely see.

With my mother making moon-cold metaphors
and my ears full of water-language.

It was a hat I had to wear
in a class she taught on laughter.

Traces of my past lives
filled with feeling beings.

I didn't want to smoke or go outside

so celebrated celibacy by dwelling on it.
In it. I took off my skirt,

left my mind.
My body nodded nicely.

WE'RE THE SAME AGE

Such loneliness impossible, I wore bells
to your funeral.

Mother said a sort of translation.

I committed memory.

Believed in watermelon.

The third hurt larger —
you can just see the words made of yoga.

All it takes is one sky, one sleepless goodbye.

Like a painting you slept, ants
disrupting the dust of your face.

You dared a vocabulary
personal as the lint in your belly button.

Numbers moved, you washed them.
Hushed them.

THE LAKE

I leave my body from the mouth like smoke.

Smiling, my brother hangs out his underwear.

On the road to thought, I hear myself singing.

A donkey converses with an angel.

*

They don't know about the wind.
Nothing can buy tenderness.
Inescapably we are
in this boat together.

ACADEMIA

Whether or not the beach is nude,
I take myself to class.
Sister, ten clouds on her back.
My beginner's mind wanders.
Unfortunate wonder.
Two teeth and I'll sell you my pearl.

So the letter from the professor arrives
while I am blowing my nose in hell.
Water and vegetables
melt into a drunk man
fumbling on the balcony.
I'll call the cops
on myself.

Over and over you say it was Spain
and I can't help but see you
as a bird again.

It's fall.
I follow you to school.

HARES

The lake gave us lip
as we limped along.

Doing peace we must be doing
something, someone

blazing on a fence, bleakest of deaths.
Skipping along, shoes torn, gold teeth.

Death's bedside manner – not all
we'd hoped but no one lies to us now.

Pills on the counter, lack-o'-faith soup.
Breadface, breadface, come out of the rain.

This farce already on page 69
of your devotions.

Still distrustful I ask you to remove
your rings and underthings.

Can't keep my legs crossed
when you doodle the infinity sign

on my knee. My earthlap.
What on it did you mean.

Your duplicitous lodgings.
They still make me blush

every time I pass the architecture building.
Blazing on a fence, I must be doing

peace to someone. Justice lightly
pausing on our cheeks, hair.

Summer just starting
to ache in my lower back.

Touch my jaw from loneliness.
I have the shivers.

A stream of lovers
climbing the hill behind the house.

A man standing in a mustard field –
From the train he is another hare.

Picture of your face
taped to my mirror.

Whatever did I mean, fast asleep,
slowly falling –

FOURTEEN MURDERS

{1}

I wanted to grab an attention.
Water! Fire!

{2}

But was too busy
being an insincere disciple.

{3}

So my sexual habits became more confused.
I'm here. I'm now.
I need a shower and some sleep.

{4}

I came from a big family.
Wasn't chosen by the translators.

{5}

The man was nervous
and nicely depressed.

{6}

Your father.

{7}

Your bitch of a father.

{8}

The sob story owned a clothing store.
I was eighteen years old.

{9}

Murder!

{10}

Because you are a fool and I once was.

{11}

Drunk, into the grave.

{12}

Your mother.

{13}

Pour me two fingers.

{14}

Water! Fire!

INNER SUBURBIA

I was married to a handsome spy.

In our house of boughs and snakes
he shook, he shat.

Balanced in our room
on hands empty and white
was an E-rated privacy.

I sat by the trampoline.
Our child was too smart to write a good poem.
Could only read book reviews.
I too doubted. In the tall garden
we came close
to being relatives,
origami doves made out of money.

Moved once a day,
not emotionally.

In uncomfortable utero.

Tiptoe   tiptoe.

WITH THE BLUE OF YOUR BREATH

One friend took the drug and became a minor deity.
The other climbed a past-life battlefield
to tend to the dead.

And if one loses a black hat and the other
buys it —

the train burns all the way to Memphis.

*

A deity on orange pillows
picks the exact chocolate,
knows how much healing coffee.

Astounding patience as we bark and lick at the stars.

In the same way that we do not question
a dream, we do not question her.

We are, we are, we are —

laughable or laudable,
fogging a mirror

in fragmented anger —
but the sun doesn't mean it that way.

The rain fringing our faces,
The rain talking back —

You make the lamp musical.

You make us ignorant in our grammar vests.

IN BREATH

Dreams of stretching – you are longer
than you know.

This might be the best I can do.

Lesbians marry on a beach,
outshine my meanness.

Apples left from last week.

I thought: *I'll just walk over to your place
and drop myself off.*

Your face a shadowed building.
Your words turn water into musk.

In the room where we made love for 200 years
I put my glasses on the windowsill,

turned off the lights with my mouth.

An awkward mind
precisely as it should be.

Past tense, yes. Pardoned.

The candles are at it again, humbly.

They have that capacity.

NEW YEAR'S DAY

I signed the contract: I will hold
on to pain. Let it burn
a tumor in my throat.
Take all parts of myself,
put them to sleep.
My good foot in hell.
Television in place of food.

We go in terror of ourselves.
Skeletons with lanterns –
We are terrorists of grand proportions.
Eating the stale history
written indifferently.
I kiss the tyrant's statue and fall to my knees.

But first let us pass through this gate
of ambitious skeletons.
Every briefcase says the same thing:
memory blotter.

You focus on the fist.

*

If I've made anything
but peace, let me sit down
on this bench and breathe
into this bottle.

Lightning cracks the jar of night.
A murdered journalist recites
from a slim volume of verse.

On the other side, in some unknown mouth,
you are counting what cannot be counted.

My friend, I am sorry
we've made war.

TINCTURE

If you carry your head in a bag
this is a blessed spot.
I don't feel like begging for the books
you borrowed. Money or leaf
we find a way.
The seal will visit and tell stories
utterly interior — who people really are
when we peel ourselves away.

Absorbed by His Black Hat

I walk with the walrus through waves of sugar. He beat me to death in
a past life. Now I can guess his middle names. Face after face. I write
them down with my left hand. A yellow bruise shivers on my forehead
— what's left of my third eye. With a blood-riddled suitcase and a
length of line he practices his play. He needs little beyond my life.
I need grapes.

Should We Treat It to Chocolate

The blood school, the bread school, the bird-ring is broken. Bring
sand from every island. We are growing into our spirits. Too close to
some shells. A green perfume I swim in. Give the canary a bath. Does
it want what we want. Velvet hair. Feather on the ground. Mangoes in
a room we run from.

I Hear Your Gender is Trendy

Grabbed a pear from the fruit shrine, kissed s/he semi-passionately, left
for school. Fingerprint clearance, orange negligee, visit from drunk
sister. Coins fell from my mouth, I became a citizen of wishfulness.

Parties

More of the same. It's winter and we eat bread. Stories inspired by a
deck of cards and too much gin. She is casual if not dead. Cookie-
stoned, admiring photographs of ice. It's often that we sit on separate
couches and wake in the same bed.

Dialogue Between Two Worlds

Funny how I feel your heart in my wrist. A toast to health, letting wealth fall beside the number eight. The musicians make myths. I'm fortunately the initiate. You dash across the street in dark clothing.

Attic Language

He left his family, wrote that he didn't need to explain his death. This was in Prague where I met the embalmer waiting by the wrong equestrian statue. She circled my street on her map. I was little more than a spirit in a bottle. Most arguments ended in a blaze.

Livings

The witch sewed. I was begging the course on Thursday. I knew all of the alphabet and some arithmetic. I was fit for falling. And fell. Shut my sister in thought. She a far-fetched carpet. To meet me flying. Blame had left my vocabulary. I ate too quickly. Falling back on my limbs. The stove she hopped it. Her eyes jewelling the night. I fought the table and forgot it. The parents' lamenting. The apparent apartment. Built closer and closer, they never starve.

Plantings

A low bin for stems. Rolling around on the blue shores. Ocean heaving. Orphans of the garden. Reclaiming their throats. Limbs and truisms. I am braying. You are slow rent. A shush breeze. From sheer laws. And who shoed you.

Frequencies She Can Dance To

Often a mushroom dish at some potluck, more likely a slide show of hikers and deer. White husky playing catch in the snow, etc. *A path of suffering*. She refers to her haircut, but can flour litter a face? Too much of a match, these women blessed by the empress of birds. With the body heat of hundreds.

Out West It's Earlier

The assassin is the dreamer in a world of prey. As child, as bird, he waited for the wrong question. Late summer, grapes bursting with sugar. The languages sounded nothing alike but he insisted that they did. Some woman threw a bar of chocolate into his train. Hunger and thirst inseparable.

There Were Lamps

I don't know who to believe: you or your hand. Going to sleep early to avoid flirting with inanimate objects. Drop a piece of bread to ensure a speedy return. I used to laugh with acquaintances.

Camping

Uneven ground. Black Cat wine, muddled understanding. In a school of birds I finally learn to sleep alone. Fallen tree = kitchen table. We stretch in the clearing you've made.

NEW SECURITY TECHNOLOGIES

Immediately when they leave
they are taken out of the system

Blue at last the sky
impossible

Night gowning us in advance

I'll paint my face

It might be appropriate

*

Iris scanners for travellers who want to fast-track

For residents of condominiums

For state employees without hands

For high-end European nightclub frequenters

*

The place is taken out/a token

An indifference to bells

My cellphone's low battery

Every monk will tell you

The place is a token

Paradise the verb

Questions

GUARD BIRDS

They say the lamp isn't human.

That a war needs maps.
Fragments and capitals.

On a recent visit to the hospital
I found him without a leg.

And she a little brighter
in death.

To make it sane
I planted poppies.

Come winter we'll be eating each other.

*

They swam out to the ship
with strings of shells,

a silver moon mask,
asking the sailors to leave.

No matter how few fruit flies we kill —

Tables held up by human backs.

Two boys and a parrot
beheaded for gold.

*

The speech writers will have him say *chance*.
I'd rather *nothing*
if that's the word you want.

A neighbour may be violent in the belly
but he is not without scent.

*

Lower us down
among the watchers.

We'll remember or we'll

forget.

DO YOU WANT TO BE A HUNGRY GHOST?

It will be very hard to hold your hand.

Death has cut your hair.

Over the bridge, I'm breathing.

I heard it would be very cold in your city –
frost at two in the afternoon.

The children melting.

Soldiers wave to the hospital.

We are another ocean
without a bed, chattering
in waves.

When so-and-so makes news,
when blah-blah dismembers the bridge –

does knowledge still glimmer?

(And if all the monkeys refuse
to climb the tree?)

THAT'S ALL WE CAN AFFORD

Hot hunger artist
in this season's latest.

This one thing never chosen
and now we're it.

What a way to make conversation.

A bit rundown – the green clock
brings us closer.

I took some apples out of the fridge.
To warm her up. To protect her.

The viper in our wallet
flew away. February.

Done. Downed.
Loaded – drink or gun.

Tell me
it's not this juvenile desk.

Sometimes hating the medium.
Dubitabilia.

A very good vocabulary
is not what I mean:

He drives me craze.

The first time animated —
you know how it is.

How we can practically
barely drink the water.

Practically, how can we.

How can we practically.

There will be drinks.
I will sleep in tomorrow.

At ten and every o'clock —

friends of friends miss us and get along.

The soldier, her hypermasculinity.

I'm a category, right?

Like the imaginary novels of the last duchess —

We don't know the names of the friends
she so desperately wants
to play with.

You didn't have your beard yet.
And birds always call late at night.

I make you up. I can't help it.

PH.D. IN CONSPIRACY THEORY

Personality – this was during a war –
and you couldn't see the place for it.

'Emotional metaphor' and the rain.
Histrionics. All-you-can-eat platter.

To stand by the sex had
on airplanes
on their way to war.

Advice:
>   – *Leave no later than ...*
>   – *Wear these shoes ...*
>   – *Say this at the gate ...*

*

Quiet and hideous, I got close
to the front.

Conducted an anti-interview with myself.
Yelled answers.

This next must be revealed
in a monologue:

Only the finest cloth. It caused
a lot of arguments
among the relatives. Of all the things
I could break today.

How interesting
to be dispensable.

Please send the 'you letters.' They've died
and they're doing okay.

BURIED WITHOUT SHOES

Meanwhile, the curious truth sidesteps
his rag doll –

A writer with a desire to please
looks confused.

The clinic is no longer a crying spa –

Time runs out from behind the door
as always

and his mother wraps up her child.

On a different morning I came to know suffering
as something important –
my body telling a story.

My village reduced to one foot.

We keep generating these lists
•
•
•
until words become worthless.

VETERANS OF THE CHILD WARS

I almost loathed another life.
All my old orphans in their beds.
The trees in their dresses – little privacy
to grieve.

A miracle made of honey and death.

In bed one month   infected uterus   cup of ash.

To inhabit the half-destroyed buildings of thought:
pitch tents.

I had been audience
witness to
reader of

wondering how best to apologize
this time.

They were busy making excuses, avoiding pain.

I was drunk, in line, a woman
with many necklaces,
a child without toes.

THE ORDER OF PERMANENT IDEAS

Bread-and-butter jobs, the simple foods
of monks.

He hadn't quite escaped yet.
His paintings show that.

Selling his library:
he had to eat.

It's completely chemical, he explained.
(His mother's suicide.)

He is remembering the cold literature
erased in a snow room.
Didacticisms while pyjamas
grew dusty.

Whatever your relationship to it,
this alphabet begins with a white dog,
a painting of a red rubber ball.

Two women wringing out time.

And vinegar, always vinegar
in the mouth.

OF THE MIRROR

the static is
very early
I will work later
exhaust
this misapprehension

*

let us choose now a pronoun

we'll be completely heaven in two hours
comprehend?

a friend's cancerous apartment
where we practice laughter yoga

we are dying really

and the sooner we discuss this ...

we disgust us

*

merely grabbing at the irreparable
as the incomparable present strolls by –
or a kind of presence
called 'ghostly'

| this spiritual 'smoking gun'

| the lighter found in mud puddle

*

later in the stadium I smoke
your last cigarette
while gazing into a fogged mirror

| rapidly my complexion fails

| your last danger this language
| we will now enter

DRONE

Overhead are monsters.

Write me a lyric for breakfast with flowers.

Dehumanizing sip
of water from a ditch.

They want/don't want to know
how it feels to kill someone.

Pressing the button with what we used to call agency.

Who is she?

Horrible computerized laughter
as soldiers step over bodies
on their way to smoke break.

Because the fathers steal more than diamonds.

A FICTION WE POSSESS

Our bloody clothes gleamed on the back deck.

We were trying to hide the crime from Mother

but all kinds of words kept creeping in.

I never understood how I became involved.

The dead man was you, was me, was she –

*

After we finished the stairs were cold.

Our magazines of war open to the bleeding jokes.

*

Put someone – any gender – in a desert

and give them a gun. Put someone behind a computer,

on a ship, in a plane, strapped to a parachute.

Put someone in a tank and say, *Go*.

Then make an excuse.

And grind it in with the palm of your hand.

DISINHERIT

People are waiting to see the herbalist – I'm glad
the window is open.

The surgeon sawing the battlefield.

Drawing in the writing class: *Hey soldier.*

Not windy today, not only
this little bright selfishness.

The clock or the phone.

Whatever the boy uses to misspell himself.

Email: redshoes@redfield.com

Closer, it's clear water.
Cold water we hate to drink.

Lonely as all over.
This boy with whom I share –

He might have whiskey, quietly
believable in the corner.

Spiritual homework to speak of.
With his winter stationery
to light this first lantern.

SHARED ROOMS

{1}

The dice. Lenin laughing.
I took the sky's girlfriend – a vase from the sea.

Solid as pieces of father's ghost.
Cancelled boats.
What you get from this

is chills. Steaks for dinner.
Promise: problem is
no problem. My girlfriend Friday.

I am cliché.
Who did you meet on the playground tonight?

Vehicular traffic – you're always confined.
Now god confides in mountain:
I'm wino. My girlfriend, wine.

{2}

Lenin climbs stairs – heaven
forgets him.

Letters from work camp:
Send blanket and some bread.

My wife memorizes suicide;
the shared room where we fry onions.

{3}

One coat, seventeen winters.

{4}

Statue of the rumpled poet
on the stairs of the museum.

Smaller now, he eats
four pieces of toast with butter.

Students gather to take his picture
in the flesh.

In Leningrad.

{5}

After, her own hands secretive.

Let the window take —
we can't.

Outside, a car idling.
Boots, hallway, thunder —

no time
to hide the papers.

THE LATTER

I wanted to be <u>hypnotized</u> so I became my father.
I found myself saying *I didn't die for this.*

It was all the same to me, sleeping
by the glass doors.

Soon there was someone who wanted to change my mind:

You've only known him in winter.
Wait until spring.

I tried to unzip my body,
found myself still part
of this wretched country.

*

When I first opened these stories
I praised death,
wrapping my legs in newspaper.

They streamed out of the yoga office.
I must have looked like a movie to them.

If a child plays a flute at night,
a snake will come.

If you love a woman, bring tangerines.

In a room you sleep, in a bed –

We put on these hard faces.

A PATRIOT

I make movies about martyrs.

A Patriot sits down. A Patriot smokes a cigarette.

Saint Beauty is a girl from elementary school.

For the heaven and hell of it.

Don't make me take off my shoes
or ever go to class again.

For the men who must be avoided
I spill my bathwater.

Grandfather was but a candlewick.

Grandmother dying and knows it well.

On the television he instructs
bruise one to succumb to bruise two.

It makes them tender on the surface.

A Patriot sleeps
through the chill of clothing.

He makes movies with his fingers.
Bow/arrow.   Limp/rain.

A boy touches the scar on his mother's stomach.

A Patriot acts.

They can call themselves 'sir' as much as they like –

a beast looks good in martyrdom.

'I HOPE SOMEONE CATCHES ME LOOKING KIND'

Beautiful Miss Peace Rally:
'We need to film us right now.'

This filter. Biting our lip.
Adjusting our death –
sooner if possible

because the good quiet girl
survives. 'I thought mean

things but didn't say them.'
Buttons left on the floor.

Words never paid for.
Peace is too dramatic for these blood

documents. *I have news*
for who do you think you're not that –

Prairie, I don't miss you
in a day of walking.

Drive until we abandon
the car. At the ocean

I'm joined by my sisters
whistling.

THEY GO IN CHASE

The goat cheese is soft.
What do you mean by a holiday.

Calling your mother back –
her earrings have rotted,
the flies are so very small.

Helicopters overhead –
spied on by the stupidest fathers.

Please bug my shower radio:

'{static} trading my {static}'
'car'
'indifference {static} explosives'
'long distant {static}'
'love distantly'

*

We frisk ourselves. The airport neutral.

*

I must be more of an expert.
Must behave/parade
my knowledge.

Kidneys full of trauma.
Throat never so angry.

Set ourselves on fire on the steps of the Big House.

Question:
Question:
Question:

The reporters in white in lime
tied and feathered –

UNFETTERED

Green and groundless, I resume.

Airplanes are not sympathetic,
launching into yesteryear.

Couch and family = stone.

Python doll, magenta tarantula.

I'm too old for this wind-up language.

'Ice storm'
'Ice house'
'Ice forget'

                    *

Your tail shimmers
in the sympathetic heat.

On the bus to the pacifist's house
you are pinstriped, eyes a storm.

How could I forget?

The slow fan, lilacs
where I slept.

Sentences don't make sense

I want to drink you
through the cup of hours

Our bandaged mothers

Faces of camouflage, of fatigue

Are we still necessary, or back in the car?

Did you return to your cousins playing tic-tac-toe?

On the day I started to shiver, you started to snow

The hole in the universe repaired
by your pocket grammar –

Of the forest we become

the yawn

CONSIDER THE COUSIN WHO PICKS UP THE PHONE

You and your friends aren't rumours
Only see two lovers a week

I dream of being
Wash my hands in wine

Death is no explanation

My dancing bandaged

I'll try not to cover my ears

*

I can think of a cold nude
Short, easily flattered

He was for years my only inspiration

My echo   my limp

Sitting with legs crossed

In love with so many at once

THE LAST PEN, THE FIRST STRAW —

                              Begin again, thorough ghost.

Gloat over other shoulders,
                              confess, collapse.

                         I like to read
about your travels – large
and tasteless oranges, someone
to distract me from myself.

In the hospital for four days,
I was the sky.
Angelic pills, wired jaw –
it was my duty to remember
the physical details.

Looking over the war schedule
these mornings of salt and anger,
                              I mirror
                              their thoughts,

look for this book in the flames.

A sigh is no explanation.
Not sentimental, not 'feminine.'

Tea lights and B vitamins –
to carry across the border.

Do the teachers help, or hide
naked in the dead woods?

Chronicles

GRAFFITI, OR, YOU ARE ON YEW STREET

We have been busy hating
& making homespun slogans.

Very busy. A canister of you
is a canister of me.

Walls: we can climb them,
knock them down, or dissolve …

Someone wants to respond,
to enter an egoless room.

You are on Yew Street
facing audio charges,

half-stepping, afraid of drama & editing.

But the undo mob isn't angry.
They're busy loving everything.

Taking fire-walking classes,
wondering if the compost worms will eat glass.

It's not just manipulations on a page.

She *let* the children throw rocks at her.

It's not just paragraphs someone wants to call emotional.

Every dog must learn repetition:

Let's go downtown & pick up some costumes!

& unlearn:

My mask – doesn't quite fit.

OUTLANDISH LETTER

Noting nothing, I want to 'express' —

Sent the package overnight.

(There will be an after-salt, something
to damage & ruminate on,
desexed streets of an altered scape.)

Of course not.

Of course:

     — Kissing the mystic parts of you, she ...

     — Dear, the landlord has married a bridge out of the neighbourhood &ₒ ...

Just as one speaking rotten
at a horse-&-tumor show.

To tame love into a note.

Restless: watering eyes, skeletons dancing in the stomach

& jubilatory liquids —

Salt collected from a ledge next to your pillow.

Mopping the room with your ugly thoughts.

Drinking a spiritualized water.

We have read the sad comments
& have said them
to excess.

Expressing sand in a glass in a beach house

a real lamp remains unlit

& we are just angrier than you. That's all.

THE BOYS IN THE TREE

But I myself am a carrier of pain.

Last night female.

Last night ghosts.

Sharing debts & dogs.

What a mother who was raped
might teach her son about masculinity.

What a mother in the middle of the night
might say about suicide.

*

I find myself thinking things.

Unfortunately blame is always
one of the options.

There are reasons for silence
on this & every other subject.

I can't think of any now

having lost a parent
& a young
age.

You have to make it right now, out of the materials at hand.

My friend said she'd been 'spiritually busy' – then danced away.

Choose to lose. Or better yet – don't play.

The most clever party fractured like a father's wrist.

When we lose all compassion, a computer takes charge of our house.

Spellcheck changes *reality* to *realist*.

The pathetic hope with which you approach all things.

An author dies & is more present in our lives.

Your text, a funeral dress.

Pack up the poem, boyhood of innocent greed.

In his introduction, in smoking jacket & cigarette:

The poet, he ...

The critic, he ...

The reader, he ...

He   he   he   he   he

I'm laughing.

SUBJECTIVE DATA

Innovating to prefer living
on fried air

& firebombing —
glass to catch

by virtue of a doorway
filling with smoke

I am guessing
you are speaking
with someone who has been traumatized

Saw blood on a door
a dawn driving away

If it is true we are paranoid
obsessed with sleep

If we heap it on
filling a doorway with spoke

Everything can be heard, made
of aggression & love

In its purest form
telling us to shut the fuck up
& sit the hell down

As a subject used to being
socially tired

In experience & inexperienced

A door blistered & whispering:

There never was a real fire at our house

THE SEXUAL

Thirst is occasionally intelligent.

One of those scars you meet on a beach.

She was a graffiti artist & recently jailed.

Some use the word *gifted*.
I never know what it means.

In a box of free books:
fault ink & grammar trauma.

Excited is a state:
Your ballroom, your bike, your gown.

Thoughts lie on top of each other.
No – nothing so orderly as this,
& dangerous, a performance.

It starts with smashing perfume bottles on the floor,
then blowing on microphones.

No one wants to talk about the erotica of the absurd –
but what sort of room spills wine like this?

You took classes on Shakespeare & dated volunteers.

She had been lying, & would continue to.

DRAFT OF AN ESSAY

Buckets of snow to melt into bathwater.

Thirsty, he enters the inn, sees birds
in a cage & frees them.

Cruel & stupid as a brain tumour.

Full of the music of dead radios.

Seaweed tattooed on each wrist.

& a bridge to get comfortable falling from.

My thesis: keep distance.

Keep a distance with me.

Bicycle buried in the snow.

We are walking.

Why bridges are necessary.

Next to a candle these sentences have no point.

In his tent

so different from me to teach kindness.

A grove of snow trees, good wine souring.

Outline: news was given,
taken away.

A judge no longer has to ponder or wonder —

The tailor now tearing the cloth.

BLAME

Cooking in a white dress.
A while dress.

It will be karma, my costume
& speech. Sister humming
son to sleep.

A gap, again,
between 'self' & 'world.'

I am this mushroom, this potato
torn from the front garden.

Also listing on the couch,
I am the dumbest theorist.

Repetition again.
Like an erotic riddle: lake, lake, water.

Theory drips; strong coffee;
coffin brashly in the rain.

Huddled over, handed in.
Before communism,
we just called it 'sharing.'

The individual can be a monstrous thing.
Like your husband's drug habit & death.

After he left, nights
of apologies: *Can I sleep next to you?*

& you: *Yes, but carefully.*
I am very afraid.

Dreamt him scrubbed, nervous,
new suit, suitcases.

Where are you going?

I don't know, but it's okay.

Every night we meditate with bones.

Mop the contagious hospital in a while dress.

Who will address this?

Like fault, you find me.

STUNNING

Medication juice, medication shake, medication's handwriting.

Trudging.

& what we lack in spirit is crude gaiety.

My juvenile guide outshines
& asks us to shrug into our father's fur coat,
to change the feared penmanship.

Silence is best if laughter not available.

By the look of your shirt, I'd say
you've been eating rubies.

It depends on how these questions are answered
but the cowards in the attic keep anticipating
the end
& stunt themselves accordingly.

A description of the song is eaten
with inexcusable bliss.

I am sleeping for days in an abandoned tank
while the soldiers plant vegetables.

There are monstrous stories being told
but it's not our gift.
It's not ours.

ANOTHER VULNERABILITY

& we're not empty, just made of air.

Sipping shadows of a cocktail.

That's we, talking to ourself.

No crash in this poet's economy of gratitude debts.

That's you, trying to turn tragedy into strategy.

Are we all critical of elegies?

Let's put on our empathy boots & write!

An imaginary bird in an imaginary cage
playing pronoun games.

This most-beloved contemporary criminal:

Hey, thanks for letting me steal
the afterlife of your novel.

As a maker of banal movies,
I love a good circle of thieves.

Here in the gutters with guitars,

freely sharing personal information,

we are trivial, difficult, unnecessary & pranksterish.

Lacking, we turn to laughter.

BEING YOUNG PROFESSIONALS

We had been writing letters,
diaries & children's stories.

Some assumed we were nuns.
None of us proceeded linearly.

We came from semi-radical backgrounds,
knew how to grow vegetables.

Our jobs were common,
of the weekday variety.

Something had happened/heightened
our awareness.

An angel painting a boy on the wall
dividing our public & private selves.

A memory of murdered parents,
the false commons of our rented gardens.

The pond in sight of the bankruptcy court
where we spotted wisdom fish.

Such details led us to believe
we were living in poverty.

We liked to read & needed a job.

To think our way out of this drowning dream.

We had to do something
& we made choices.

THE WAR THEATRES

Loss of the current
self

Connecting with the eating others

The armed forces
The arm-me

Used to think I had a good memory
Not 'good memories'
but the ability to remember

Three months: I took up arms

Seven: thought war, felt spiritually confused

Ten: whispering the horrifying reproach

I know that – in this city, at least –
you can call someone

You can engage in sexual boasting
& make dreams out of the residues of the day

Sometimes the bad feelings are just hunger

The mystery a simple bullying story

& sometimes they are the difference
between safe naked
& naked naked

A guide weak & terrified
tortured into leading

A phone book opened to the burning page

A deck of cards, a bird, a lion

Someone in the audience standing up
& walking away

STARE

Mother said not to worry.

I was picking up teeth from the ground so carefully.

Hired to help rebrand the military.

I was picking up small pieces.

The crow kept landing on a branch near my window.

There was nothing heroic about it.

I kept writing, fashioning images.

My family ate tangerines that week.

At night, the cries of city owls &

Mother appears dead in my dreams,
then flying

with a lit paper
to torch newspapers.

She was it now – the embodied, the war
we'd been avoiding.

Never can I see her eyes, only sense

her silence like paper tigers burning
in the cold houses off Main Street.

Nieces' voices, cousins' empty shoes —

all our relations
waiting at dawn train stations.

In the hollows of the week
there is still time.

There are still bones
burning in the ash.

READING

Naming names, gaming games.
A snarl of pillows.

Crows are assembling
on my fake pot belly.

My elaborate beard.
I don't know what you heard.

I heard he was a talented youth.
Tangible details like air in your lungs.

I heard you stop trying not to.

A goat is eating poetry & lemons.
I have been knowing tattoos.

Burnt edges of an open book
& responsible details – too personal

to be embarrassing.
Like the yarn of my cousin's socks.

Everything goes on too long.
Doctrine, bacteria.

Orange juice I thought was constructed.

My comfort lies in these stories
so burn them.

DANCE

The rain's small hands. Your logic
shining – it makes no
human sense.

To gather – they are coming – together.

We have missed a beat, find each other
at the apocalyptic disco.

We can buy ready-made love songs
like a dream of wearing girl shoes.

When you die, all your thoughts
left hovering in the air.

This recommendation letter written by a ghost.

Authority has an 'author' in it,
& there is always the possibility
that when someone calls your name –
you don't turn around.

A suitcase can be filled with money
& so can your mind.

A being might begin.
In our own neighbourhood.

In the streets of this or that thought.

You might move. You might move
someone.

NOTES AND ACKNOWLEDGEMENTS

'Subjective Data': The final line is Dora speaking in Freud's *Fragment of an Analysis of Hysteria (Dora)*.

'Dance': The first line is a riff on e.e. cummings' famous final line of 'somewhere I have never traveled, gladly beyond.'

To these and any other sources I have borrowed from, my gratitude.

'Of the mirror' was written after reading Robin Blaser's essay 'The Irreparable,' and is dedicated to his memory.

'Draft of an Essay' is dedicated to the memory of Chawn Brown/Carrie Gill.

'Blame' is dedicated to the poet Heather Lane, with thanks.

Thank you to Margaret Currin for introducing me to the work of Giannina Braschi.

Thanks also to the Canada Council for the Arts for a grant that gave me time to work on this book.

Grateful acknowledgement to the editors and readers of the following publications in which some of these poems first appeared: *Apocalypse Anthology, Burnside Review, Cream City Review, dandelion, dig, Event, Good Foot, Hayden's Ferry Review, Interim, Konundrum Engine Literary Review, Lungfull!, Matrix, Mississippi Review, No Tell Motel, Ocho, Pistola, Salt Hill, The Fiddlehead, Verse*.

For their help with this book I'd like to thank: my editors at Coach House, Kevin Connolly and Alana Wilcox; my partner-in-life-and-writing, Christine Leclerc; and the poets of the now-defunct collective vertigo west, who gave feedback on some of these poems. Thanks also to Evan, Christina and all the other folks at Coach House for their work.

This book couldn't have been written without the love and support of my community. To my dear friends and beloved family: your bright spirits make me want to keep living. Thank you.

ABOUT THE AUTHOR

Jen Currin has published two collections of poetry, *The Sleep of Four Cities* (Anvil Press, 2005) and *Hagiography* (Coach House, 2008). She lives in Vancouver, B.C., where she teaches writing and literature.

Typeset in Montrachet and Linotype Didot
Printed and bound at the Coach House on bpNichol Lane, 2010

Edited by Kevin Connolly
Designed by Alana Wilcox
Cover art by Christine Leclerc
Cover design by Christine Leclerc and Rick/Simon
Author photo by Sarah Race Photography

Coach House Books
80 bpNichol Lane
Toronto ON M5S 3J4
Canada

416 979 2217
800 367 6360

mail@chbooks.com
www.chbooks.com